Common Core Lessons & Activities: Scientific Method

By Carole Marsh
Published by Gallopade International, Inc.

Printed in the U.S.A. (Peachtree City, Georgia)

TABLE OF CONTENTS

G: Includes Graphic Organizer
GO: Graphic Organizer is also available 8½" x 11" online download at www.gallopade.com/client/go
(numbers above correspond to the graphic organizer numbers online)

Scientific Method

Read the text and answer the questions.

Scientists study the natural world around them. There are several important tools that scientists use to investigate the natural world. They can make observations by using their five senses—sight, hearing, smell, taste, and touch. They can research facts that have already been discovered and collected in books, journals, illustrations, maps, online resources, and other sources. Scientists can take measurements and perform experiments to test their ideas about the natural world. Scientists use reason and logical thinking to find answers and draw conclusions.

All of these ways of learning about the world are tools used in the scientific method. The scientific method is a series of steps that helps people think logically about the natural world and understand it better. The steps of the scientific method help people clearly question, test, and compare ideas in a factual way.

The scientific method is not just for scientists. The scientific method encourages everyone to ask questions, think critically, and understand the natural world. The scientific method helps all kinds of people—students, teachers, businesspeople, explorers, and doctors, for example—to think critically and to learn more about how the world works and why things happen.

1. Summarize information from the text to answer each question.
   A. What is the scientific method?
   B. Who uses the scientific method?
   C. Why is it used?
2. Explain why the scientific method is often called a process of "investigating the natural world."
3. List at least five "tools" that scientists might use to investigate.
4. Which of the following would NOT be part of the scientific method? Why?
   a) drawing conclusions by using reason
   b) asking a friend's opinion
   c) thinking critically about observations
   d) questioning and testing an idea

MAIN IDEA

In the Past

Read the text and answer the questions.

Long ago, ancient people observed natural forces like storms, eclipses, and volcanoes but did not know why they occurred. They did not use the scientific method to study and explain the natural world. Instead, ancient people claimed that these natural forces were caused, or controlled, by gods, goddesses, fairies, and other supernatural forces.

The scientific method changed the way people understand the natural world. The first scientists were people who explained natural events using reason and logical thinking. They closely observed nature and began to see patterns. They noticed that storms are caused by patterns of wind and temperature. They saw that eclipses could be explained by the motion of the Earth and Moon around the Sun. They began to see that volcanoes were not caused by an angry god, but by movements of the Earth's crust.

Scientists use the scientific method to solve many mysteries of the natural world. However, there are still many mysteries that have not yet been solved. Today, branches of science like biology, geology, and astronomy study different parts of the natural world. They all use the scientific method to increase our understanding of how and why the natural world works the way it does.

1. Place a ✓ next to the statement that best summarizes the main idea. Support your answer with evidence from the text.
   a) _____ Ancient people believed in gods and goddesses.
   b) _____ Scientists use the scientific method to explain nature.
   c) _____ The scientific method changed the way people understand the natural world.

2. A. Use a dictionary to define supernatural.
   B. What two ways of thinking helped scientists to disprove the idea of supernatural forces?

3. **True** or **false**: Science aims to investigate the causes of events in nature.

4. What is the purpose of branches of science today?

Steps in the Method

Read the text and answer the questions.

The scientific method has six basic steps. The first step is to ask a question. People are curious, and it is normal for them to ask questions about the world and how it works. For example, you might want to know, "Why is the sky blue?"

The second step takes some effort: research. Research can involve reading about a subject, experiencing it firsthand, talking to knowledgeable people about it, and finding photos or illustrations. Research is anything that someone does to learn about a subject.

The third step involves using reason, knowledge, and even imagination: construct a hypothesis. A hypothesis is a possible explanation that could lead to an answer for the question. For example, a hypothesis for the question "Why is the sky blue?" is that it is filled with blue water.

The fourth step is often the most fun: conduct an experiment. The experiment should be designed to test whether the hypothesis is true or not. To test the hypothesis that the sky is filled with blue water, someone might go up in a hot air balloon to see if they can touch or feel the water in the sky.

The fifth step requires thought: analyze the results. Once the experiment is complete, the results are written down and studied. The hot air balloon rider would find that there are no pools of blue water in the sky. But, he or she might have discovered that the sky has both air and water vapor (gas). These results show that the rider's first hypothesis was incorrect.

What happens when the hypothesis is incorrect? The scientific method follows the saying, "If at first you don't succeed, try, try again." Go back to step three and come up with a new hypothesis and conduct another experiment. Most scientists go through many hypotheses and experiments before they find answers to their questions.

The sixth and final step of the scientific method is important to everyone: report the results. Whether the hypothesis proved true or false, the results add to human knowledge about the world around us. The next person who asks the question will be able to build on the discoveries of scientists who came before.

PART A: Complete the sentences with the appropriate underlined vocabulary word from the text.

1. People do _______________ to learn about things they want to know.
2. If you are curious about the world, you will ask many _____________.
3. ________________, or think about, what you have seen and learned.
4. Scientists conduct ____________ to test what is true and what is not.
5. You share your knowledge when you _______________ your results.
6. It takes imagination to develop a _____________, or possible answer.

PART B: Number the parts of the scientific method in the correct order.

7. _____ Construct a hypothesis
8. _____ Analyze the results
9. _____ Ask a question
10. _____ Report the results
11. _____ Conduct an experiment
12. _____ Research the topic
13. If the experiment proves the hypothesis incorrect, go back to Step _______.

PART C: The following statements are examples of steps in the scientific method. Label each step, and number them in the correct order.

<u>**No.**</u> <u>**Step**</u>

14. ____ ______________ Read a library book about water. Find an online source that explains the properties of water.
15. ____ ______________ Write out everything you thought and did. Post it on the classroom blog.
16. ____ ______________ Ask: why is the water in our fish bowl so low?
17. ____ ______________ Measure the water level in the fish bowl. Cover it with plastic wrap for two days.
18. ____ ______________ Maybe some of the water evaporated into the air.
19. ____ ______________ See the condensation on the plastic wrap. Measure the water level in the fish bowl. Think about what happened.

Asking Questions

Read the text and answer the questions.

1) Asking questions is the first step to learning about the world. As scientists observe the world around them, they want to know how things work, what causes things to happen, and how things can be changed. People ask many questions, but only some questions can be answered by the scientific method.

2) A scientific question is one that can be researched and tested to be true or false. For example, "What happens to the salt in saltwater when the water evaporates?" or "Do soybeans grow faster if music is played near them every day?" These questions could be researched or tested to discover factual answers.

3) Some questions do not need the scientific method to get an answer. They are verification questions and can by answered by collecting data. Verification questions are very useful to science but they do not have to be tested by the scientific method. Examples of verification questions could be, "What color are my shoes?" or "How tall is the soybean sprout?" These questions can both be answered by observation or measuring.

4) Some questions cannot be answered by following the scientific method. For example, "Should I wear the blue or red dress today?" or "Do you like chocolate chip cookies better than oatmeal cookies?" These questions are based on opinion, which changes from person to person. Opinions are not fact and cannot be researched or tested.

1. Place a ✓ next to the sentence from the text that most clearly states the main idea.
   a) ____ Asking questions is the first step to learning about the world.
   b) ____ People ask many questions, but only some questions can be answered by the scientific method.
   c) ____ Opinions are not fact and cannot be researched or tested.
2. A. What qualities define a scientific question?
   B. Write an example of a scientific question.
3. A. Explain why verification and opinion questions are not appropriate for the scientific method.
   B. Write an example of a verification question.
   C. Write an example of an opinion question.

Questions: Broad & Specific

Read the text and answer the questions.

Questions can be either broad or specific

Broad questions are undefined and have many possible answers. A broad question could be "How does sound affect plants?" Broad questions like this are difficult to answer using the scientific method.

Specific questions are defined and precise. A broad question like "How does sound affect plants?" can be narrowed down to be more specific and defined. What type of plant? What type of sound will you play for the plants—music or noise? If music, what type of music will you play—classical, hip hop, rock, or jazz? How loudly or softly will you play the music? How long will you play the music each day? How long will the experiment last?

An example of a specific question could be "Do soybeans grow faster if loud, classical music is played near them 12 hours a day for one month?" This question is well defined and clearly explains what will be tested by the scientific method.

1. Match each word to whether it describes a broad (**B**) question or a specific (**S**) question. Use a dictionary if necessary.
   A) _____ defined B) _____ undefined C) _____ narrow
   D) _____ precise E) _____ vague F) _____ wide

2. Compare and contrast the example question in the first paragraph to the example question in the third paragraph. How are they similar? How are they different?

3. Place a ✓ by each question that is specific. Rewrite each question that is too broad to be more specific.
   A. ________ How do plastics affect living things?
   B. ________ Do goldfish grow larger if they receive at least an hour of sunlight each day?
   C. ________ Are loud sounds dangerous?
   D. ________ Do two objects of the same mass fall at the same rate?
   E. ________ Do red M&Ms melt faster than brown M&Ms in direct sunlight?

Research

Read the text and answer the questions.

Once you have a question, the next step is to do research. Research is the process of gathering information that is already known. Scientists research the basic information that they need to know before developing a hypothesis. For example, Thomas Edison did not discover everything about electricity. He studied the work of many scientists before him and applied that knowledge to build the electric light bulb.

There are five important steps for effective research. First, gather information on the topic you are interested in. Textbooks, newspapers, and scientific journals are great tools for research. The internet is a great source of information, too. However, it is important to only gather information from online sources that you can trust. Some internet sources have incorrect information.

Second, read through the sources you have gathered. Third, summarize the main idea and supporting details that are important. Write down basic information that relates to your specific question. You do not need to write everything you have read.

Fourth, classify the information by noting any similarities and differences in what you have read. For example, if you read about the effects of loud music on living things, be sure to note whether the effects were seen in plants or animals, and whether the music was classical, jazz, or rock. It is often helpful to classify information by making a chart, table, or a graph. Fifth, cite, or record, your sources by listing the author's name and where you found the information. This lets other people know where you found the information.

1. A. Use the text to define research.
   B. Why do scientists do research?

2. Create a table to summarize the five steps for doing research. Identify each step, describe what it is, and explain its purpose.

3. A. Make a list of all the research tools available in your classroom.
   B. In your opinion, which research tool is the most useful? Explain.
   C. Why should you be careful when researching information from the internet? As a class, discuss the pros and cons of using the internet.

Gathering Knowledge

Read the text and follow the research prompts.

Scientists share their knowledge by recording their discoveries in books, and by giving speeches and reports to other scientists. The work of scientists in the past is important to the work of scientists today. Scientists study the work of previous scientists, test their ideas, and improve on their scientific knowledge.

Thomas Edison / Michael Faraday

Abel Niece de Saint-Victor / Marie Curie

Bernhard Riemann / Albert Edison

Joseph-Marie Jacquard / Herman Hollerith

Jean-Baptiste Lamarck / Charles Darwin

PART A: Work together with a partner or a small group. Choose one of the pairs of scientists above.

PART B: Gather two or more reliable online resources. Check with your teacher to see if the websites are reliable and accurate.

PART C: Read through the information you have gathered and take notes to summarize the important information. Use the following questions, as well as three of your own, to guide your research.

A. What subject did both scientists work in?

B. What scientific contributions were made by each scientist?

C. Did the work of one scientist affect the work of the other? Explain.

PART D: Organize your information into a digital presentation. Include visual images and explain the relationship between the two scientists. Cite your sources at the end of your presentation.

PART E: Give your presentation to your class. As a class, discuss the following questions aloud.

1. How does present-day scientific knowledge build on past knowledge?
2. Why is it important to question the work of scientists who came before you?
3. Does a scientist's hypothesis have to be correct to contribute to scientific knowledge? Support your answer with evidence summarized from the class presentations.

Construct a Hypothesis

Read the text and answer the questions.

A hypothesis is a possible explanation to a question or problem. Scientists do not just "dream up" a hypothesis. They gather evidence from their observations, research, and experience to develop a plausible answer to their question. A plausible hypothesis is one that is reasonable or could possibly happen.

The hypothesis is not always an answer—it is one of many possible explanations. A hypothesis is not a guess—it is an explanation that is supported by evidence from observation or data. A hypothesis is not an opinion. Unlike an opinion, a hypothesis is testable so it can be proven true or false.

After constructing a hypothesis, scientists design an experiment to test the hypothesis. Experiments are used to gather data and results as evidence to support the hypothesis. If the evidence does not support the hypothesis, a scientist can revise, or change, the hypothesis and design a new experiment. Often, a scientist will revise his or her hypothesis many different times before finding the right explanation to answer the question.

1. A. Use the text to define hypothesis.
   B. How is a hypothesis different from a guess?
   C. How is a hypothesis different from an opinion?
   D. What steps of the scientific method help a scientist develop a hypothesis? Which step helps a scientists test a hypothesis?
2. Define the word plausible by giving a synonym and example.
3. Read the **question** and the two possible hypothesis—**H1** and **H2**.

Question:	"Why do we only see the sun in the daytime?"
H1:	A fiery chariot carries the sun across the sky every day.
H2:	The Earth rotates on its axis and the sun is only visible to people while their side of the Earth faces it.

   A. Which hypothesis could be tested scientifically?
   B. Which hypothesis cannot be tested scientifically?
   C. Which hypothesis is more plausible? Explain why.
   D. What evidence supports the plausible hypothesis?

EXPERIMENT ANALYSIS

Galileo's Experiment

Read the text and answer the questions.

Through most of the 1500s, many scientists thought gravity caused heavier objects (objects with more mass) to fall faster than lighter objects (objects with less mass). In 1589, the Italian scientist Galileo did not believe this, and he performed an experiment to try to prove this theory wrong.

Galileo got two metal balls, one heavy and one light. Then he and his students went to the leaning tower of Pisa, where Galileo had decided he would perform the experiment.

Galileo carried the balls to the top of the tower, while his students remained down below to observe. With great concentration, Galileo dropped the two balls at exactly the same time. Galileo's students on the ground carefully watched as the balls fell through the air.

The two balls hit the ground with a thud at the same time. Observers noted that the heavier ball made a deeper dent in the soft ground, but it did not fall any faster.

1. Place a ✓ next to the statement that best summarizes the purpose of Galileo's experiment.
   A) _____ To prove that gravity pulls objects to the ground.
   B) _____ To show that experiments are necessary to test new ideas.
   C) _____ To prove objects dropped from the same height fall at the same speed, regardless of mass.
2. List items you would need in order to recreate Galileo's experiment.
3. A. Write step-by-step instructions to perform the experiment.
   B. Include tips for safety in your instructions.
4. List at least two likely reasons that explain why Galileo conducted his experiment in front of an audience.
5. A. Why did Galileo use two balls that had different weights?
   B. Why did Galileo drop the two balls at exactly the same time?
6. A. Write a hypothesis that reflects Galileo's point of view.
   B. Was Galileo's hypothesis shown to be correct or incorrect?

Scientific Method Chart

Write in the name and definition of each of the scientific method's 6 steps, in order, in the graphic organizer.

1

2

3

4

5

6

Fill in each step of the scientific method in the correct place in the flow chart. Explain what scientific "tools" you might use in each step. Tools may be ways of thinking or specific scientific equipment.

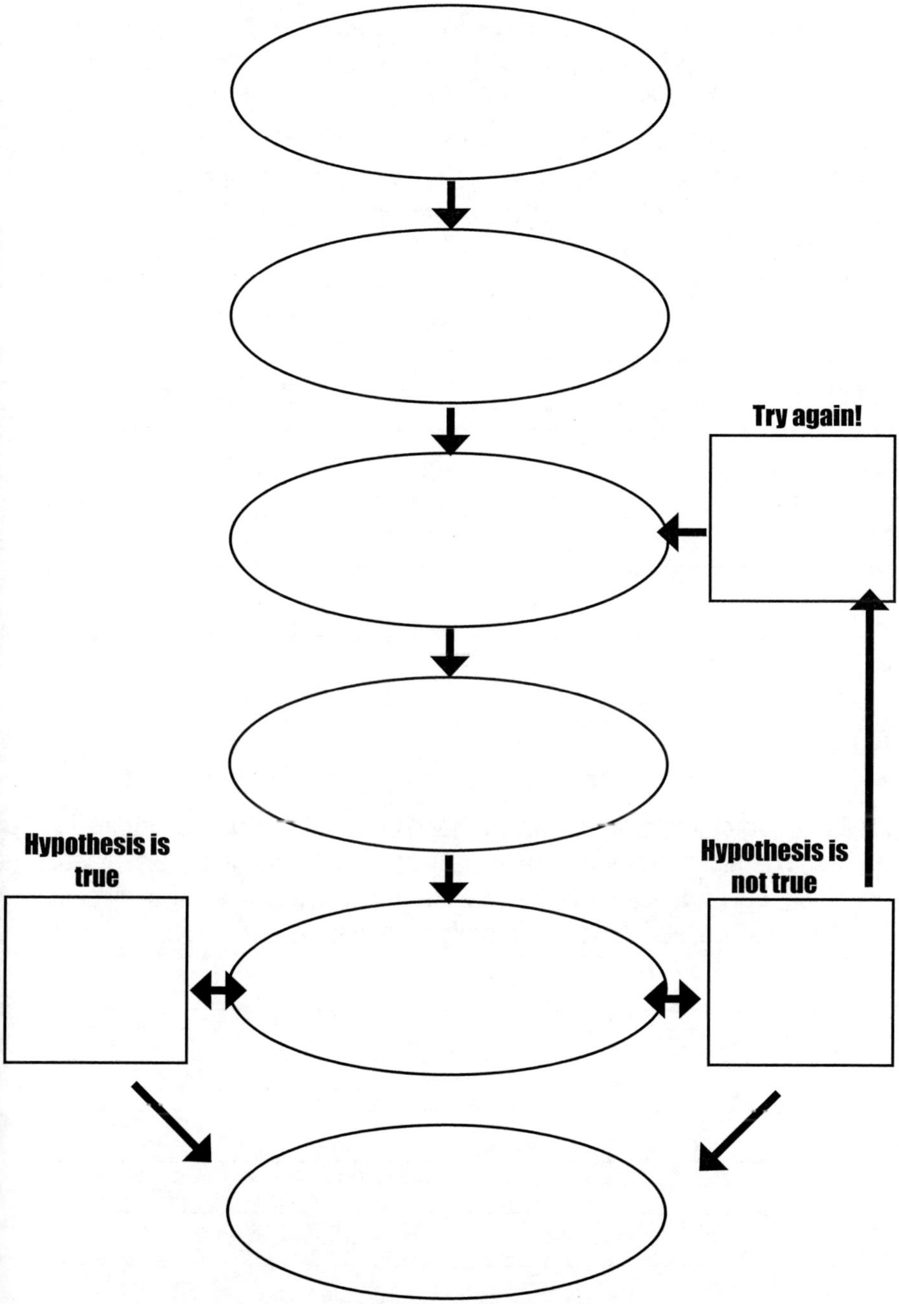

Use Your Senses

Read the text and complete Parts A and B.

A scientist's five senses are the most important tools of observation. Scientists use their senses to see, hear, taste, smell, and touch things when asking questions. They use those same senses to observe and experience the results of their experiments.

PART A: Choose one of the 10 objects and observe it using all of your senses. Complete the table by recording your observations.
Important note: not all items should be tasted!!!!!

apple • feather • pencil • saltine cracker • rock • water
tree leaf • paper • shell • M&M

SENSE	ITEM:____________________ Description
Sight	
Hearing	
Taste	
Smell	
Touch	

PART B: Some experiments involve loud noises, laser beams, sharp objects, chemicals, and other potentially harmful substances. List at least one thing that could damage each sense organ. Then infer what pieces of equipment scientists could use to protect each body part.

eyes ____

hands _______________________________________

hair ____

ears ____

nose____

body____

Quality vs. Quantity

Read the text and answer the questions.

Data comes in two forms, qualitative and quantitative. Qualitative data is best explained as a "description." A quality can be observed but cannot be measured. Colors, textures, smells, tastes, and more, are examples of qualitative data. Quantitative data is best explained as data that can be measured in numbers. There are many different types of quantitative data, including height, weight, length, width, area, volume, and more.

1. Use the text to complete each sentence with the correct vocabulary word.
   A. She took note of the animal's ____________________ data by recording how tall it was and how heavy it was.
   B. She took note of the animal's ____________________ data by recording how its fur looked and felt.

2. Identify each of the following observations of a bean sprout as either **qualitative data** or **quantitative data**.

   A. 2 leaves ________________________________
   B. short, wide leaves ________________________________
   C. slight scent ________________________________
   D. non-poisonous ________________________________
   E. 13.75 centimeters tall ________________________________
   F. bitter taste ________________________________
   G. 25% growth in 1 week ________________________________
   H. thin, delicate stem ________________________________

3. Determine whether each example is a change in **quality** or **quantity**.
   A. _________ After a week, the plum's smooth skin became wrinkled.
   B. _________ Out of a class of 24, two students stayed home sick.
   C. _________ The carpenter sawed 17 centimeters off a wood beam.
   D. _________ A tree's green leaf changes color in the fall.

Writing Prompt

Write two paragraphs about yourself. Title the first paragraph "My Qualitative Data," and include at least 4 examples of qualitative data about yourself. Title the second paragraph "My Quantitative Data," and describe at least 4 examples of quantitative data about yourself.

Standard Measurements

Read the text and answer the questions.

It is important that scientists share information in ways that are understandable for everyone. That is why measurements are standardized, or made the same, around the world. Standard measurements are important for doing experiments and recording data. Scientists need information to be consistent to make sure that experiments are always done with the right measurements.

Most standard scientific measurements use the metric system. The metric system starts with a basic measurement, called a base unit. Scientists add prefixes to each basic unit to change its value. Each prefix is a factor of ten. For example, "kilo" means "thousand." (1 kilometer = 1,000 meters)

1. A. Define the word standardized as it is used in the text.
   B. Why do scientists use a standardized system?
2. Complete the chart by adding the prefix to each basic unit.

Prefix	Meaning	Symbol	Length	Mass	Volume
kilo-	Thousand (1,000)	km		kilogram	
hecto-	Hundred (100)	hm	hectometer		
deka-	Ten (10)	dkm			dekaliter
Base unit	One (1)	m	meter	gram	liter
deci-	Tenths (0.1)	dm		decigram	
centi-	Hundredths (0.01)	cm			
milli-	Thousandths (0.001)	mm			milliliter

3. A. Circle the base units of length, mass, and volume
   B. How many meters is 1 hectometer?
   C. How many decigrams is 1 gram?
   D. How many liters is 1 kiloliter?
4. Choose the best measurement of distance between two cities. Explain why this measurement is most useful.
   a) kilogram b) kilometer c) centimeter d) milliliter

PROBLEM-SOLUTION-RESULTS

The Slime Experiment

Read the text. Then complete the graphic organizer by summarizing the text, and answer the analysis questions.

Dr. Snailus noticed that three of her favorite pet snails were suffering from "the slime." She knew that if the snails were left untreated, they would eventually die from the slime. Dr. Snailus knew that fish also suffer from the slime. Using an online resource, Dr. Snailus found that some fish can be cured by rubbing seaweed on their bodies and some fish can be cured by using medicine.

Dr. Snailus thought, "Perhaps the same methods used on fish will also cure my snails of the slime." For 1 week, she rubbed the 1st snail's shell with seaweed once a day. She gave medicine to the 2nd snail once a day. Dr. Snailus left the 3rd snail alone so she could compare the results of the other two snails with a slimy snail. After 1 week, the 1st snail was slime-free, the 2nd snail became sick and died, and the 3rd snail remained slimy.

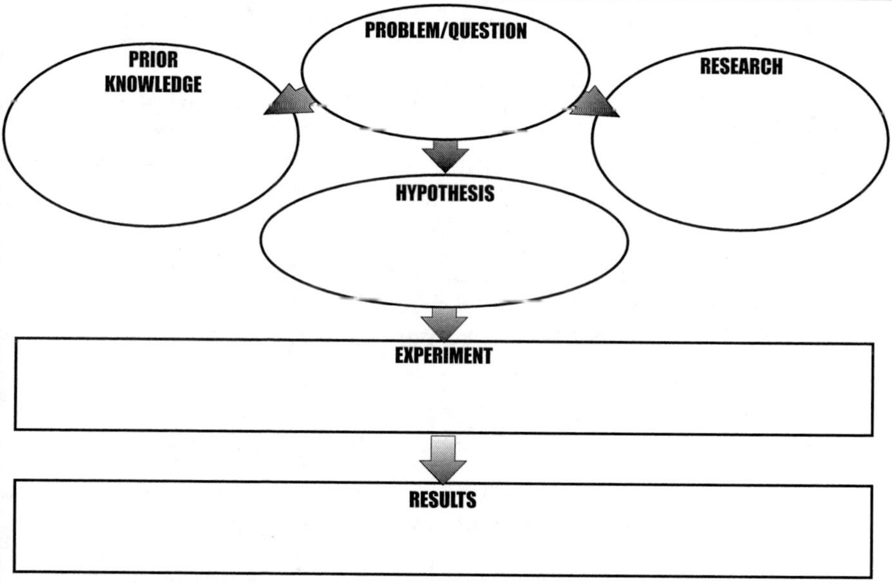

Analysis Questions

A. Was Dr. Snailus' hypothesis proven correct or incorrect? Cite evidence from the text to support your answer.

B. If incorrect, explain how Dr. Snailus might revise her hypothesis.

Experiment: Variables & Controls

Scientists use experiments to discover causes and effects, and learn why things happen in nature. The purpose of an experiment is to study something under controlled conditions. By controlling what affects the experiment, scientists can observe which factors cause things to happen and which factors do not.

What is a variable?

A factor that changes is called a variable. For example, imagine you are trying to determine the best way to cook brownies. The obvious variable is temperature. Another variable might be whether the oven uses gas or electricity. Scientists only test one variable at a time to clearly see which variable causes the change.

There are two different kinds of variables—independent and dependent. An independent variable is a factor that is usually considered a "possible cause" of some effect. A dependent variable is a result of the independent variable. Most experiments have many factors that remain constant. A constant is a factor that is carefully kept the same each time the experiment is repeated.

Test against a control

When conducting an experiment, it is important to have a control. A control is a test subject that does not get exposed to the variable. Controls make it possible to see how the variables affect the subject and to measure the results.

PART A: Use information from the text to answer the questions.

1. Match each description to the word from the text it defines.
   A. A test subject that is used for comparison
   B. The effects of changing an independent variable
   C. The part of the experiment that a scientist purposefully changes
   D. Factors that a scientist keeps the same at all times
   E. Any part of an experiment that experiences a change

2. A. Is an independent variable most similar to a **cause** or **effect**?
   B. Is a dependent variable most similar to a **cause** or **effect**?

3. Controls help scientists clearly see what effect a variable has in an experiment. Infer why it is important for scientists to test only one variable at a time. Write a paragraph explaining your answer.

PART B: Read the text and answer the questions.

I believed that music causes plants to grow taller but did not have proof. I also thought that a plant's height might vary depending on what type of music was played.

I chose three soybean plants as my test subjects. I planted the soybeans in three separate containers with the same amount and quality of soil. Every day, all three plants were watered and received the same amount of sunlight. Two of the plants, I exposed to music for 24 hours a day. I moved one soybean plant to a room where loud rock music was played, and I moved the other soybean plant to a room with soft jazz music. I placed the remaining plant in a quiet room with no music.

At the end of 8 weeks, I measured, photographed, and described each plant. The "quiet" plant measured 12.5 centimeters, the "rock" plant measured 14 centimeters, and the "jazz" plant measured 14.5 centimeters.

Then, I wrote an essay. I included photographs of the plants' growth and explained how different types of music affected the plants. I then published my findings in a scientific magazine.

4. Use the text to determine which paragraph describes each of the following parts of the scientific method

   A. _____ report
   B. _____ experiment
   C. _____ analysis
   D. _____ hypothesis

5. A. List at least three factors that are held as constants.
   B. Which plant is considered the control—quiet, rock, or jazz plant?

6. Complete the graphic organizer by identifying the independent and dependent variables. Describe the effects of each independent variable on the two plants exposed to music.

Variable 1		Effect on Height
Rock	→	
Variable 2		**Effect on Height**
Jazz	→	

7. A. Was the author's hypothesis proved or disproved?
   B. What conclusions can the author draw about the effects of music on plants?

8. A. Why might it be important that the author mention what type of plant he tested in his experiment?
   B. If the author used three different types of plants, would the experiment results be invalid? Explain why or why not.

Sound and Pitch

Pitch is the highness or lowness of a sound produced by a vibrating object. Several different factors affect the pitch of an object.

Look at the data from each experiment and answer the questions.

Experiment 1 (used finger to pluck objects)	Object	Distance stretched	Pitch observed
	Thick rubber band	5 centimeters	low pitch
	Thin rubber band	5 centimeters	medium pitch

1. A. What factor was the variable in Experiment 1?
   B. What factor was held constant in Experiment 1?
   C. Analyze and summarize the results of Experiment 1.

Experiment 2 (used finger to pluck objects)	Object	Distance stretched	Pitch observed
	Thin rubber band	5 centimeters	medium pitch
	Thin rubber band	10 centimeters	high pitch

2. A. What factor was the variable in Experiment 2?
   B. What factor was held constant in Experiment 2?
   C. Analyze and summarize the results of Experiment 2.
   D. Compare and contrast Experiment 1 with Experiment 2.

Experiment 3 (used metal fork to strike objects)	Object (volume)	Volume filled (water)	Pitch observed
	Glass bottle (100 ml)	10 milliliters	high pitch
	Glass bottle (100 ml)	50 milliliters	medium pitch
	Glass bottle (100 ml)	90 milliliters	low pitch

3. A. What factor was the variable in Experiment 3?
   B. What factor was held constant in Experiment 3?
   C. Describe how the variable affected pitch.

Experiment 4 (used metal fork to strike objects)	Object	Diameter	Length	Pitch observed
	Tin pipe	1 centimeter	10 centimeters	high pitch
	Tin pipe	1 centimeter	50 centimeters	medium pitch
	Tin pipe	1 centimeter	90 centimeters	low pitch

4. A. What factor was the variable in Experiment 4?
   B. List two factors held constant in Experiment 4.
   C. Analyze and summarize the results of Experiment 4.

5. What part of each experiment was a dependent variable?
   a) object b) distance stretched c) pitch observed

PRIMARY SOURCE ANALYSIS

An Inventive Experiment

The text is an excerpt from Alexander Graham Bell's journal.

Read the text and answer the questions.

Mr. Watson was stationed in one room with the receiving instrument. He pressed one ear closely against S and closed his other ear with his hand. The transmitting instrument was placed in another room and the doors of both rooms were closed.*

I then shouted into M the following sentence: "Mr. Watson—Come here—I want to see you." To my delight he came and declared that he had heard and understood what I said. I asked him to repeat the words. He answered "You said 'Mr. Watson—come here—I want to see you'." We then changed places and I listened at S while Mr. Watson read a few passages from a book into the mouth piece M. It was certainly the case that articulate sounds proceeded from S. The effect was loud but indistinct and muffled; If I had read beforehand the passage given by Mr. Watson, I should have recognized every word. As it was, I could not make out the sense—but an occasional word here and there was quite distinct. I made out "to" and "out" and "further" and finally the sentence "Mr. Bell do you understand what I say? Do—You—Un-der-stand—what—I—say" came clearly and intelligibly. No sound was audible when the armature S was removed.*

**M is a device for speaking into.*
**S is a device for listening.*

1. What step of the scientific method is Bell describing?
2. What step of the scientific method was Bell performing when he wrote the page in his journal?
3. Use the information from Bell's page to infer:
   A. His question
   B. His hypothesis
4. Was Bell's experiment successful or unsuccessful? How do you know?

Tools of a Scientist

Use a dictionary or online resource to define each characteristic of a scientist, and explain why each characteristic is important to the scientific method.

	Characteristic	Definition	How might it help an scientist?
A	inquisitive		
B	persistent		
C	creative		
D	logical		
E	open-minded		

1. List at least three other characteristics a scientist might need.
2. Match each characteristic from the chart to the quotation that best describes it.
   ________________ "The ultimate authority must always rest with the individual's own reason and critical analysis." – *Dalai Lama*
   ________________ "Imagination is more important than knowledge." – *Albert Einstein*
   ________________ "Curiosity is the wick in the candle of learning." – *William Arthur Ward*
   ________________ "I was taught that the way of progress was neither swift nor easy." – *Marie Curie*
   ________________ "For me, it is far better to grasp the Universe as it really is than to persist in delusion, however satisfying and reassuring." – *Carl Sagan*

Sharing Your Opinion

PART A: In your opinion, is the scientific method a helpful way to understand why things naturally happen? Explain why.

PART B: Use what you have learned about the scientific method to write a persuasive essay **for** or **against** the scientific method. Give at least five reasons supporting the scientific method OR five reasons against the scientific method. Support your opinion with reasoning and examples.

PART C: Summarize the main points of your essay into a short speech explaining why you do or do not support the scientific method.

PART D: Give your speech to the class. Can your audience accurately identify your point of view?

Correlations to Common Core State Standards

For your convenience, correlations are listed page-by-page, and for the entire book!

This book is correlated to the Common Core State Standards for English Language Arts grades 3-8, and to Common Core State Standards for Literacy in History, Science, & Technological Subjects grades 6-8.

Correlations are highlighted in gray.

PAGE #	READING	WRITING	LANGUAGE	SPEAKING & LISTENING
	Includes: RI: Reading Informational Text; RST: Reading Science & Technical Subjects	*Includes:* W: Writing; WHST: Writing History/Social Studies, Science, & Technical Subjects	*Includes:* L: Language; LF: Language Foundational Skills	*Includes:* SL: Speaking & Listening
2	RI RST . 1 2 3 4 5 6 7 8 9 10	W WHST . 1 2 3 4 5 6 7 8 9 10	L LF . 1 2 3 4 5 6	SL . 1 2 3 4 5 6
3	RI RST . 1 2 3 4 5 6 7 8 9 10	W WHST . 1 2 3 4 5 6 7 8 9 10	L LF . 1 2 3 4 5 6	SL . 1 2 3 4 5 6
4-5	RI RST . 1 2 3 4 5 6 7 8 9 10	W WHST . 1 2 3 4 5 6 7 8 9 10	L LF . 1 2 3 4 5 6	SL . 1 2 3 4 5 6
6	RI RST . 1 2 3 4 5 6 7 8 9 10	W WHST . 1 2 3 4 5 6 7 8 9 10	L LF . 1 2 3 4 5 6	SL . 1 2 3 4 5 6
7	RI RST . 1 2 3 4 5 6 7 8 9 10	W WHST . 1 2 3 4 5 6 7 8 9 10	L LF . 1 2 3 4 5 6	SL . 1 2 3 4 5 6
8	RI RST . 1 2 3 4 5 6 7 8 9 10	W WHST . 1 2 3 4 5 6 7 8 9 10	L LF . 1 2 3 4 5 6	SL . 1 2 3 4 5 6
9	RI RST . 1 2 3 4 5 6 7 8 9 10	W WHST . 1 2 3 4 5 6 7 8 9 10	L LF . 1 2 3 4 5 6	SL . 1 2 3 4 5 6
10	RI RST . 1 2 3 4 5 6 7 8 9 10	W WHST . 1 2 3 4 5 6 7 8 9 10	L LF . 1 2 3 4 5 6	SL . 1 2 3 4 5 6
11	RI RST . 1 2 3 4 5 6 7 8 9 10	W WHST . 1 2 3 4 5 6 7 8 9 10	L LF . 1 2 3 4 5 6	SL . 1 2 3 4 5 6
12-13	RI RST . 1 2 3 4 5 6 7 8 9 10	W WHST . 1 2 3 4 5 6 7 8 9 10	L LF . 1 2 3 4 5 6	SL . 1 2 3 4 5 6
14	RI RST . 1 2 3 4 5 6 7 8 9 10	W WHST . 1 2 3 4 5 6 7 8 9 10	L LF . 1 2 3 4 5 6	SL . 1 2 3 4 5 6
15	RI RST . 1 2 3 4 5 6 7 8 9 10	W WHST . 1 2 3 4 5 6 7 8 9 10	L LF . 1 2 3 4 5 6	SL . 1 2 3 4 5 6
16	RI RST . 1 2 3 4 5 6 7 8 9 10	W WHST . 1 2 3 4 5 6 7 8 9 10	L LF . 1 2 3 4 5 6	SL . 1 2 3 4 5 6
17	RI RST . 1 2 3 4 5 6 7 8 9 10	W WHST . 1 2 3 4 5 6 7 8 9 10	L LF . 1 2 3 4 5 6	SL . 1 2 3 4 5 6
18-19	RI RST . 1 2 3 4 5 6 7 8 9 10	W WHST . 1 2 3 4 5 6 7 8 9 10	L LF . 1 2 3 4 5 6	SL . 1 2 3 4 5 6
20	RI RST . 1 2 3 4 5 6 7 8 9 10	W WHST . 1 2 3 4 5 6 7 8 9 10	L LF . 1 2 3 4 5 6	SL . 1 2 3 4 5 6
21	RI RST . 1 2 3 4 5 6 7 8 9 10	W WHST . 1 2 3 4 5 6 7 8 9 10	L LF . 1 2 3 4 5 6	SL . 1 2 3 4 5 6
22	RI RST . 1 2 3 4 5 6 7 8 9 10	W WHST . 1 2 3 4 5 6 7 8 9 10	L LF . 1 2 3 4 5 6	SL . 1 2 3 4 5 6
23	RI RST . 1 2 3 4 5 6 7 8 9 10	W WHST . 1 2 3 4 5 6 7 8 9 10	L LF . 1 2 3 4 5 6	SL . 1 2 3 4 5 6
COMPLETE BOOK	RI RST . 1 2 3 4 5 6 7 8 9 10	W WHST . 1 2 3 4 5 6 7 8 9 10	L LF . 1 2 3 4 5 6	SL . 1 2 3 4 5 6

For the complete Common Core standard identifier, combine your grade + "." + letter code above + "." + number code above.

In addition to the correlations indicated here, the activities may be adapted or expanded to align to additional standards and to meet the diverse needs of your unique students!